Big Game Hunters & Closers

a GoalsGutsGlory title

Big Game Hunters & Closers

Attract and Keep Your Super Sellers

Alice Wheaton

Jellicle Ball Publishing Company

an imprint of CoreGrowth Foundations Inc.

Published by Jellicle Ball Publishing Company
an imprint of CoreGrowth Foundations Inc.
Suite 1844, Westhills Town Center
Calgary, Alberta T3H 3C8
CANADA
www.alicewheaton.com
Toll Free: 1 (877) 542•5423

GoalsGutsGlory™
is also a registered trademark of CoreGrowth Foundations Inc.

National Library of Canada Cataloguing in Publication Data

Wheaton, Alice, 1951–
    Big game hunters & closers

ISBN 0-9730366-0-5

1. Sales personnel. 2. Sales management. I. Title.
HF5439.5.W43 2002   658.3'044   C2002-910559-5

Series ISSN: 1703-3888

CREDITS
Editing: Wayne Magnuson, Prairie House Books, Calgary, Alberta.
Series cover design, interior design & project management: Jeremy Drought,
    Last Impression Publishing Service, Calgary, Alberta.

Printed and bound in CANADA by Friesens, Altona, Manitoba.

Dedication

JOHN CARSTAIRS *helped me define my vision, build a stronger personal core, and establish a long-term strategy and foundation for my business. For his patience during multiple editing sessions, generous sharing of ideas, and profound knowledge, I dedicate this book to John.*

Anything worth doing is worth doing imperfectly. To be more successful, we must be willing to make more mistakes (p. 61).

Acknowledgements

VERY FEW AUTHORS create a book without the generous support of others. I would like to acknowledge Lisbeth Cormier, who owns a home-and-office maintenance company. Her willingness to help me in ways that go beyond her job description has been a tremendous support. I am in awe of her. Aine Curran's strategic advice has tempered a rash move on my part more than once! Lorraine King was the first to encourage me to write, and I appreciate her continued support. Elaine Evans, who tested my ideas and freely shared her success stories with me, kept the tap of encouragement flowing. I am also grateful to Hazel Scott, who read my manuscript in the early stages and then kindly agreed to read it again. Although I have known Aldon Snyder only a short time, the work he does for me helps me to do a better job in my own work, and I appreciate that.

Another person who has influenced me with his wit and wisdom is my teenage son, Lloyd Worth. He graciously discusses with me the work that I do. Casey, my black cat, helps me relax by sitting on my papers and laptop, thereby forcing me to take a break.

Finally, my gratitude overflows to the person who changed my life completely, Bill Irwin, the sales manager at Xerox who agreed to hire me. I had no previous sales or business experience, yet he taught me the skills of Big Game Hunting and Closing. He encouraged me to hold nothing back, to be as successful as I

There's more to motivation than positive thinking; we need the ability to move forward in the face of negative thinking, overwhelming fear, discomfort, doubt and insecurity (p. 56).

could be. This book, and other titles in the series, are a natural outcome of his guidance.

Alice Wheaton,
Calgary, Alberta
June 2002

Contents

Introduction

*Big Game Hunters and Closers—they're
emotionally charged, limitless, and always in control.*

J UNIOR AND MIDDLE SALESPEOPLE are in abundant supply,
but there are only a few Super Sellers. They are
known as *Big Game Hunters and Closers*, and
companies are struggling to attract them and keep them.

Standing out from the crowd is serious business: the
difference is leadership. Alpha leaders survive regardless
of conditions. Alpha male and female wolves lead the
pack because they are the strongest members. They
ensure the survival of the pack, even through difficult
times. Big Game Hunters and Closers are "Alpha Sellers."

A sales team composed of Big Game Hunters and
Closers stands out from the crowd. The team is
successful because every member has the ability to sell
in adverse conditions, even when the competition has a
product or service that is of equal or superior quality.

Big Game Hunters and Closers generate a steady
supply of income for their company and in so doing

Big Game Hunters and Closers…provide the CEO with something to sell – performance, the essence of the company – to bankers, brokers, employees, and shareholders.

provide the CEO with something to sell—*performance, the essence of the company*—to bankers, brokers, employees, and shareholders.

Big Game Hunters and Closers differentiate themselves from the gatherers, whose focus is building relationships rather than searching for new business. Building relationships is good, as far as it goes, but it doesn't go far enough. If their agenda is to practise *relationship selling*, salespeople lose track of the primary purpose: to provide a solution to the client and the company as a whole, not just to be liked by the contact.

Many relationship sellers make a contact within a company and become stuck at that level, afraid to go above the contact for fear of losing the relationship. Meanwhile, the competition, who is a Big Game Hunter and Closer, has connected with the real decision maker and closed the deal. Alpha Sellers can do both: create a steady income and build strong business relationships.

Big Game Hunters and Closers have the discipline to do what so many junior and middle salespeople don't want to do. They are willing to pay a price for success. They operate on the basis of mastery versus perfection, and they are mentally tough.

This book shows you how to attract, develop and keep Big Game Hunters and Closers—the Super Sellers—on your sales team.

Attract and Keep Your Super Sellers

CORPORATE STAKES ARE HIGH. To survive, you need to be able to sell. The best product in the world is soon a burden if you cannot sell it.

The extent to which a company can sell its product or service determines the size of the dividend checks and shareholder bonuses. To survive—and thrive—you need to be able to attract and keep Super Sellers.

There's an old adage in the sales industry: *Buy 'em or build 'em*. In other words, you can hire Super Sellers or you can develop them.

One of the advantages to buying Super Sellers is speed. They drive new business quickly because they can hit the ground running and stay revved up.

One disadvantage to hiring top salespeople is that Alpha Sellers are aware of other competitive companies that would gladly give them an opportunity. It is also evident that there is an abundance of salespeople at the junior and middle levels. Alpha Sellers know their own value, which is reflected in the remuneration packages they expect. A signing bonus often precedes opening any A-list doors.

Once seduced by the salary, bonuses, stock options and other perks, Alpha Sellers don't stop searching. It is in their nature to continue the prowl for bigger and better opportunities.

The alternative is to *build* a top performer. It will take longer, but the results can be worth the investment in time and training. When you *develop* a person into a Big Game Hunter and Closer, there are benefits in two key areas: your salary and benefit costs are lower, and you won't have to offer as many perks or a signing bonus to have them on your team. There is also less risk that they will be *poached*.

In my experience, it is wiser to *build* the Big Game Hunters and Closers, and this book will teach you how to do that.

Positive Deviants

The word *deviant* usually carries a negative connotation. In this instance, however, deviant is positive. Positive deviants are those salespeople who excel in their roles by deviating from the norm.

To illustrate, let's look at school grades. The norm (average) is a grade of *C*. Anyone receiving a *D* or *E* is showing a negative deviation from the norm. Students who receive *B* or *A* grades are showing a positive deviation from the norm.

The deviants we are most interested in are those who fall in the *B* and *A* grouping. Alpha Sellers are found within this area of the bell curve.

The character traits of positive deviants (Levels 4 and 5) are significantly different from those in Levels 1, 2, and 3. To understand these differences, please study the following graph and selling behaviors.

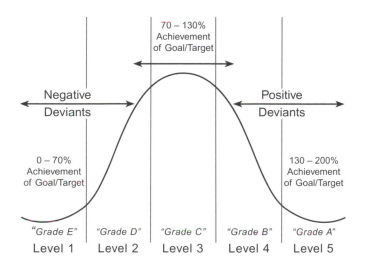

Positive deviants are those salespeople who excel in their roles by deviating from the norm.

Level 1 Selling Behavior

The Level 1 Salesperson

- Intends to become a vendor only.

- Focuses only on the product/service to be sold/delivered.

- Maintains a casual *pursue*, *capture*, *disengage* mentality when dealing with clients.

- Turns the product or service into a commodity by using price as the main selling factor.

- Tends to be more comfortable selling to front-line buyers or end-users.

Mental State: *Unconscious Incompetence*
They don't know what they don't know.

Emotional State
Level 1 salespeople are worried primarily about survival, so every action or any change in their methods is about their struggle to survive. The Level 1 salesperson is quick to point to others or some outside force as the root of his/her lack of success.

Level 2 Selling Behavior

The Level 2 Salesperson

⚙ Intends to close the deal.

⚙ Places some focus on the customer.

⚙ Has learned how to develop some trust.

⚙ Can understand applications and solutions that the product or service provides.

⚙ Sells products or services to those who work at the supervisory level.

Mental State: *Conscious Incompetence*
They know they don't know it all.

Emotional State
Caught early, Level 2 salespeople maintain a sense of humility which, simply put, means they can be taught to be Alpha Sellers. They are accepting of feedback about mistakes they've made and, more importantly, they are open to advice from those who have more experience.

Level 2 salespeople carefully sift through all of the data to find the changes that would most benefit their sales portfolio. They are not likely to spend their time defending or justifying lackluster performance, but are willing to open their minds and learn a new method, procedure, or process.

The open-mindedness of Level 2 salespeople, combined with a thirst for power, can lead to the pursuit of excellence and improved sales techniques. The result is a highly motivated individual who rises rapidly through the positions, often becoming one of the top salespeople on the team.

CAUTION! Some Level 2 selling behaviors are misleading. Only a few candidates have Super Seller potential.

The Level 2 salesperson who moves up to Level 3 will choose one of two roads:

- **Road X**: He or she may reach an average performance level but not move forward from there.

- **Road Y**: The individual becomes extremely motivated to move forward and become a Super Seller, thus becoming a positive deviant.

Level 3 Selling Behavior

The Level 3 Salesperson

- ✪ Intends to become a long-term supplier and provide excellence to win clients and gain repeat business.

- ✪ Is concerned about competition from other suppliers or service providers and develops competitive strategies proactively.

- ✪ Explores product/service issues within the competitive climate and deals with problems before risking the loss of a client.

- ✪ Sees the value in a reciprocal relationship. They are beginning to think in terms of finding win-win agreements to secure and maintain business.

- ✪ Is able to sell products and services to upper management. These individuals are polished in their approach and are more likely to get their foot in the door to meet with upper management.

Mental State: Unconscious Competence
Level 3 salespeople are consistent in their approach. They are average and dependable performers who are not consciously aware of their abilities.

...open-mindedness...combined with a thirst for power, can lead to the pursuit of excellence and improved sales techniques.

Emotional State

Unconscious competence is dangerous because it is accompanied by a certain amount of effortless success. Unfortunately, this can lead to an attitude of arrogance. Once this happens, Level 3 salespeople resist reminders to be humble, their minds are closed to new ideas, and they are nearly impossible to teach or train.

Salespeople at this stage also risk becoming story tellers who reflect on the glory days, when they were dazzling the world with their sales knowledge, skills and charm.

Unconscious competence is also dangerous because its victims lack the ability to leverage knowledge. They can't synthesize and transfer their knowledge, skills and attitudes to others. Not everyone can be a teacher or mentor. Level 3 salespeople believe that training means having the trainee observe what they do.

Not to be underestimated, the subconscious mind can lead people to sabotage. Consider *your* willingness to teach someone everything you know if you thought it might result in losing clients, sales or perhaps even your job?

The tendency to withhold and defend knowledge serves to limit the progress of a salesperson. Defending one's own knowledge base precludes benefiting from the knowledge of others, while the dissemination of knowledge produces the power of leverage.

Level 3 salespeople will often begin training recruits by saying, "Just come with me on a call and watch what

I do." The problem with this approach is that trainees will not know which behaviors to observe. Having no point of reference, they do not benefit from the knowledge of the Level 3 salesperson. The bottom line and potential income are affected negatively because the new recruits have not been taught to sell effectively.

People at Level 3 are also hindered by their inability to create a strategic sales plan. Instincts are what drive the Level 3 salesperson—the emotional framework based on the power of their personality and presence.

Requirements of Big Game Clients

Current conditions require that Big Game clients are forced to do more with less. They are challenged intellectually with technological demands, and they work in highly competitive business environments. At one time, competition meant selling more than the next company. Today, decision-makers face mergers, hostile take-over bids, and global competition.

When a company chooses a supplier, the salesperson must fulfill many expectations. Level 3 salespeople are unable to satisfy the expectations of Big Game clients. Although a winning personality is an asset, it is not the primary criterion for becoming the supplier of choice.

Defending one's own knowledge base precludes benefiting from the knowledge of others, while the dissemination of knowledge produces the power of leverage.

Level 4 Selling Behavior

The Level 4 Salesperson

- ✪ Knows that Relationship Selling is ineffectual without special attention to the task.

- ✪ Creates a strong solution for the needs of clients to gain *insider status* with each client. Salespeople at this level see themselves as consultants who know how to combine the needs of the client with their hunger to succeed.

- ✪ Is able to perform highly sophisticated assessments (e.g., internal communication audits, focus groups) thus providing solutions for an entire company instead of just one department.

- ✪ Has well-evolved skill levels and experience, and can leverage that to participate in strategic planning with key customers.

- ✪ Is vigilant to ensure the client's needs are being met, including attention to detail and minor changes.

- ✪ Recognizes the needs of clients and understands that he or she must *qualify* to provide services or products to any given company. The importance of this is not lost on the salesperson who has gained long-term contracts from the same clients year after year, and will re-qualify for current and upcoming opportunities.

✪ Asks the client what they want and need, knowing there is no relationship if it is not reciprocal. Level 4s are adept at asking to be the customer's supplier of choice. By the same token, they will ask the client what is expected of the service or product.

✪ Knows that database management is not the same as nurturing client relationships. Knows clients cannot be managed; they can be nurtured by design, not by default.

Mental State: *Conscious Competence*

Level 4 salespeople are accomplished. They are mentally alert, emotionally fit, and they are committed to being lifelong learners. They are always aware of the fact that they don't have all the answers. They are also a pleasure to have in a training session because their EGO, which can be an acronym for Edging Goodness Out, doesn't prevent them from being open to diverse ideas. They interact freely with the group and have a general interest in others' learning, as well as their own.

To Super Sellers, focus is everything...and because they have a concrete, sequential understanding of their success, they have a system for management and measurement.

Emotional State

To people with conscious competence, focus is everything, and success is the only option open to them. Because they have a concrete, sequential understanding of their success, they have a system for management and measurement. It may not fit with the company's system, but they do indeed have one.

Level 5 Selling Behavior

The Level 5 Salesperson

- ✪ Has all of the attributes of a level-four salesperson, and more.

- ✪ Knows what to do when winning and what to do when losing.

- ✪ Sustains long-term processes for developing and maintaining win-win negotiations.

- ✪ Establishes pre-contracting, where they ask the client for a series of incremental commitments leading to the final contract.

- ✪ Looks for opportunities and new clients, which contributes to the success of the sales team and the bottom line for the company.

- Pre-qualifies and re-qualifies to avoid unrealistic expectations of people and/or outcomes.

- Creates a priority list within the client base, and lets lower priorities go to junior salespeople without feeling guilty.

- Taps into the good graces of others for referrals to more A-list clients.

Mental State: *Conscious Vigilance*

Level 5 salespeople know the cost of achieving this level of success, and are willing to pay the price. They are vigilant in acquiring new skills and wisdom. Knowing that new skills can come from unexpected sources, they are neither arrogant nor closed-minded. You will never hear them say with disdain, "I already know that."

Emotional State

Level 5 salespeople appear to glide through life, with business coming to them. Standing in their own circle of power, they are most comfortable with others who also have an aura of power. They are masters at showing up bigger than they feel, because they know they must constantly rise to new challenges.

To people with conscious competence, focus is everything, and success is the only option open to them.

The Power of a Weakness

By the time we are in our late 20s and early 30s, we have tapped into core strengths that we can use to achieve goals. Few people realize that our weaknesses are also a source of potential strength and success.

Level 4 and 5 salespeople monitor their own progress and make changes as needed. They can teach what they know with logic and reason, and so have leveraging power. They can hire an assistant and double or even quadruple their success. They are vigilant about knowing their fears and weaknesses because they have learned a very important secret: unlimited potential arises from recognizing a weakness and transforming it into a strength.

When a weakness is identified and a plan of action is consistently implemented, a new strength emerges. Level 4 and 5 salespeople are familiar with this process. They know that anything worth having is going to cause a certain amount of pain. To think otherwise is to have a naive personality, rife with magical thinking.

Case Study

Carlos, a stockbroker, had been employed with a company for a mere seven months when he attended my workshop, *Prospect and Prosper: Cold Calling Strategies that Work Even for Chickens, Cowards, and the Faint of Heart*. Carlos had a goal of managing $10 million in assets within his first year at the company—before he was to lose the guaranteed financial base. This put fear into his heart because a great portion of his business development activity was focused on prospecting and cold calling. When he picked up the phone he also picked up fear, doubt, and insecurity. With these feelings, and with only five months to go, he couldn't see how he'd survive without the guaranteed base.

After attending the workshop, he contracted me to work with him on his drawbacks. Carlos and I had three separate meetings, and within three months his portfolio increased by $5 million. However, he did all the work by himself. He had developed the willingness to feel uncomfortable while in pursuit of his goals. Urgency and desperation can be highly motivating!

Recently the sales manager at Carlos's firm left the company to explore new opportunities at another brokerage firm, hoping to take his clients, or at least his client list, when he left the firm. Carlos and I had our first meeting just after the sales manager had resigned. The

When a weakness is identified and a plan of action is consistently implemented, a new strength emerges.

VP of Sales had given Carlos and the other members of the sales team a portion of the client list to contact.

The old feelings of procrastination, defending, and justifying began to return, but after facing his fears, Carlos recognized and counteracted these behaviors. He was no longer dominated by the fear of asking for what he wanted.

Step One

Working together, we created a script for Carlos to use when he started making calls to clients on his list. At first he used the script imperfectly, but by adjusting his presentation he was able to reduce his hesitation time and adapt the script as needed. Carlos achieved an amazing feat. He contacted every client on the list and, for those he could not speak with, he left a voice-mail message. Even more impressive: every person returned his call because of the powerful message he had left.

Step Two

The next challenge was for Carlos to return to the VP and ask for more clients. We agreed that he would ask the VP by saying, "I've contacted every client you gave me, set appointments with some and left messages for others, and now I want to make more cold calls."

This was a bold step and we knew that the VP would take issue with his asking for more names on the client list. We predicted the VP would say he had to be fair to the others on the sales team, and that is exactly what he said. Carlos handled this objection gracefully by replying, "Of course, I understand you want to be fair. I'm sure you also want to secure as much business for your team as possible. If you ever have clients that you want to hand over to me, I'll be sure to call them immediately. Please think about it."

Result: Just two days later, the VP handed Carlos a client list with a potential $3.5 million. Carlos had demonstrated by his actions that he had the ability to be an Alpha Seller.

Step Three

The next challenge was for Carlos to go back to the VP and tell him he wanted even more clients to call. When I introduced this challenge, Carlos went through a wide range of emotions, which we named and addressed so they would not become obstacles.

First, his disbelief: "Oh, I can't do that. I'll feel sheepish, like I'm begging for business." Second: "What if he gets annoyed with me?" And third: "It isn't very nice of me to edge out my peers."

The need to be liked can rob us of much in both business and personal pursuits. One of my own philosophies was never more important than at that particular moment. I said, "We miss out on 100% of what

The need to be liked can rob us of much in both business and personal pursuits.

we don't ask for; the answer to our question will always be *no* if we don't ask."

Result: Carlos implemented the plan, even while feeling trepidation about what he was going to ask for. He was amply rewarded. A week later he sent me an e-mail saying he was completely occupied with meeting new clients until the end of the month. Eighty percent of the total client list had chosen to go with him.

Carlos was willing to feel uncomfortable and pay the price in order to achieve his goal. And achieve it he did! I provided the tools and inspiration; Carlos provided the motivation and action that led to success.

The *old* Carlos would experience the emotions (the fears) and procrastinate, hoping that time would relieve his anxiety. The *new* Carlos moves into action, acknowledging and expressing a wide range of emotions, but not one of those emotions limits his success.

2

Leading the
Big Game Hunters & Closers

SALESPEOPLE WHO STRIVE to have more than their share of A-level clients require special leadership traits in their managers. CEOs need to be aware that their sales managers must know how to attract, develop, and keep Big Game Hunters and Closers.

A case in point is a multinational transportation company. My first contact with the company was with the director of sales, who assured me she had the financial authority to make a decision about hiring a sales consultant and trainer. Instead of making a unilateral decision, she asked me to set up an appointment with the sales manager in order to be congruent with their corporate culture, by which she meant the involvement of all concerned.

I spent two sessions with the sales manager and performed a sales audit. We identified several gaps in their sales methodology—processes that he believed should receive some intervention. We agreed that he would debrief with the director of sales, and establish priorities to close the gaps and increase business.

Weeks went by with no contact from the sales manager so I reconnected with the director, who validated my assumption. That is, the sales manager was feeling intimidated because if he took my proposal to the executive team they would say, "But isn't it *your* job to deliver this sales guidance to the team? Why should we hire an outside consultant when we have you as a sales manager?"

This sales team is at risk. If the sales manager was keeping this information from the executives, he probably keeps other information from them as well. Sales managers like this are protecting their ego instead of addressing problems and searching for solutions, for themselves as well as for their team members. If the sales manager is unable to operate from an Alpha-leader position, it is impossible for this company to develop the majority of their sales team into Super Sellers.

The director of sales must make one of two choices: either support the sales manager with the training he needs or replace him with someone who can do the job. Allowing him to continue in denial may lead to the downfall of her own career and compromise the profitability of the company.

Addicted to the Positive

Executives may be reluctant to take a hands-on approach if company culture tells them to nurture team spirit at all costs. Keeping a bad hire because s/he is "better than no one" says little for the company's reputation in the industry. It is also demoralizing to other employees who want more training and direction from their sales manager but none is forthcoming.

I received the following e-mail message after a presentation to The Executive Committee Ltd. (TEC) group. In a few words it tells a memorable story: "Alice, your comments about addiction to a positive mental attitude really hit home this week. I decided to demote my VP of Sales and Marketing to an account rep position. He had established a consistent pattern of delusional thinking about forecasts and even results. It is critical that I acquire the right talent going into 2002."

For the record, I want to say that many boards of directors, CEOs, executive team members, and sales managers are often afflicted with an addiction to positive thinking. I am not advocating negative thinking. I *am* advocating reality thinking. We all remember the demise of high-tech companies that failed to meet their brilliant forecasts. Eventually the piper must be paid. It is far better to receive bad news and create a strategy to solve a problem, which might lead to the sale, than to have *happy ears* and go under.

...many boards of directors, CEOs, executive team members, and sales managers are often afflicted with an addiction to positive thinking.

Fear of Economic Insecurity

Fear of economic insecurity perpetuates economic insecurity. I do a piece of research with almost all the sales groups I speak to at various conferences. I ask this question: "What will your sales manager say if you tell him, *Boss, I think we are going to lose this order*"? Their summary response is "My sales manager will reprimand me by saying *If you think you will lose it then you will*."

What nonsense! Sales reps need to strategize with their manager, but his/her fear of economic insecurity, combined with poor management and training skills, stands in the way. A sales leader interested in perfectionistic, positive mental gymnastics, without a base in reality, is a guarantee for sales failure. Why would a Big Game Hunter and Closer stick around?

Awareness at All Levels

Ensuring the company has its fair share of Big Game Hunters and Closers is a matter of concern for all of the stakeholders, including the CEO, the vice-president of sales, and the sales manager. Since it is the CEO who eventually sells the essence of the company to the shareholders, banks, and brokers, it is imperative that the CEO be involved in the *heartbeat* of the company: SALES.

The other problem with management is their ignorance of performance standards for Super Sellers.

Without knowing the selling behaviors of Level 4 and 5 salespeople, it is impossible to evaluate appropriately, to establish a training plan, or to correct inappropriate action. For example, few sales managers know the nine steps to core competency in cold calling and prospecting. When all of the steps are performed, the salesperson will successfully open new client doors.

...it is imperative that the CEO be involved in the heartbeat of the company: SALES.

3

Performance Standards for Big Game Hunters & Closers

HERE IS A TYPICAL ADVERTISEMENT found in weekend newspapers by companies hoping to hire Super Sellers.

WANTED: SALES REPRESENTATIVE

We are searching for a Sales Representative to join our independent Sales Team. The ideal candidate will have an established record of accomplishment in sales, will have good communication skills, and will be good with people.

The problem with this advertisement is that it's indistinguishable from countless other ads in weekend newspapers, and it's non-specific. This same advertisement could also be used for a clerk at a local fast-food franchise. Don't employers want all employees to have good communications skills and be good with people?

Survey of Employers

After reviewing page after page of advertisements for salespeople, we at CoreGrowth Foundations Inc. recently answered forty such advertisements, not to apply for the position, but to inquire about the qualifications of their sales staff. The objective of our research was to compile a list of all the requisite skills for professional sales representatives.

In the letter, my business associate explained that over the past twenty-five years he has developed, and continues to develop, career-training programs for industry, colleges, and technical institutes. The first step in developing such programs is to create an occupational profile that identifies all of the skills required for a particular occupation. Those skills are then used as the foundation for the curriculum of the training program.

My associate asked employers to state what they had identified as the skills required of a salesperson, from basic selling to super-selling.

Required Skills

The findings of this research indicate that employers do not have a clear vision of the day-to-day skills required of a successful sales representative. While occupational profiles exist for virtually every other profession, from veterinary assistant to commercial baker, from locomotive engineer to interior designer, it seems that no one has

While occupational profiles exist for virtually every other profession...no one has yet developed a comprehensive and realistic profile of the skills required of a sales professional.

yet developed a comprehensive and realistic profile of the skills required of a sales professional.

One company replied that the personal attributes required are excellent interpersonal skills, such as communicating, listening, and customer empathy. Another respondent analyzed the skills of the sales professional into three main areas: prospecting, presenting, and closing. Both of these replies, and many others, are naive and shallow in terms of the real complexity of professional selling. Prospecting is a general area of competence, but within the prospecting competency are many individual skills.

Unable to specify the skills required of a new member of their sales team, many employers abdicate their responsibility by stating "candidates must have a successful track record in sales," as if past success in one sales position is all that is necessary for future success, regardless of the industry, product, service, territory, or financial climate.

Value of Sales Occupational Profiles

Employers need a detailed and accurate sales occupational profile in order to hire new staff, conduct performance appraisals (other than a review of sales figures), and prescribe appropriate training and professional development.

A detailed and accurate sales occupational profile is the prerequisite to a meaningful job description that includes duties, responsibilities, skills, and performance standards for a specific position.

Without a detailed job description there cannot be a fair and honest appraisal of a salesperson's performance—with job expectations—or a reasonable recommendation for relevant training and professional development.

While sales training programs are in abundant supply, no two are alike. If training programs were based on a realistic analysis of the skill requirements of the selling profession, they would surely have more than a few elements in common. The fact is that too many training programs focus on motivational platitudes that do not further skill development, and too few of them are based on an analysis of the skills required in the sales profession.

Value of Job Descriptions

Without a meaningful job description, hiring is a best-guess process serving neither employer nor employee.

Without job descriptions that identify required selling skills and standards, how can employers hire people who stand a reasonable chance of success in their profession?

Without job descriptions that identify required selling skills and standards, how can sales representatives have their performance appraised fairly?

Without job descriptions that identify required selling skills and standards, how can employees select and undertake relevant training?

Without a meaningful job description, hiring is a best-guess process serving neither employer nor employee.

It is no wonder that staff turnover and levels of frustration for both employers and employees are high. With an accurate profile of competencies and skills, corporations are more likely to be successful by design than by default.

Developing a Sales Occupational Profile

CoreGrowth Foundations Inc. used three major steps in developing an occupational profile to support the sales profession in the following tasks:

❂ Recruiting new employees

❂ Evaluating employee performance

❂ Selecting relevant training and professional development

In the *first step*, a facilitator skilled in the occupational profiling process conducted a workshop with fifteen competent sales professionals from a variety of industries. Their task was to identify the areas of general competence for sales representatives, and to subdivide each general area into specific skills. This information was organized in a structural chart called the "Draft Sales Occupational Profile."

In the *second step*, a larger group of sales professionals reviewed and validated the draft profile.

Comments offered through the validation process were collected, and changes and additions were made to the draft profile.

In the *third step*, a group of sales managers specified performance standards for the listed skills. This last step is vital in developing standards specific to your industry. This cannot occur unless the foundation of general competencies and skills is in place.

The completed sales occupational profile, consisting of requisite skills and performance standards, will help managers achieve goals that have long been unattainable because there was no system for measurement or management.

Three Main Goals

Managers will achieve three main goals from developing precise occupational profiles:

1. Accurate and complete job descriptions

The benefit of having accurate job descriptions is that advertisements will better reflect the position and skill expectations. Applicants are therefore more likely to have the skills desired by the employer. The interview process can be focused more precisely on the position, and each candidate can be more accurately assessed in terms of the skill requirements.

With an accurate profile of competencies and skills, corporations are more likely to be successful by design than by default.

2. Objective and meaningful performance appraisals

Performance appraisals must be based on objective skill performance rather than on subjective evaluation. Performance appraisals will be regarded as fair and meaningful if the employee and the supervisor reach a common understanding about skills and performance standards at the beginning of an appraisal period.

3. Relevant, skill-oriented training programs

Skill deficiencies identified in the improved performance appraisal process can be addressed through specific training and professional development. Training programs can be designed to address the specific skill requirements for the job and the individual.

While waiting for a precise sales occupational profile, the sales industry has lost business and respect. Sales professionals now have a tool to assist with job descriptions, performance appraisals and training programs.

Occupational profiles and performance standards support all levels of the sales industry. The CEO is supported because the right people are hired for positions. Productivity increases because gaps in standards can be identified and remedied by appropriate intervention. And the sales team—with more Big Game Hunters and Closers—becomes successful by design instead of by default!

4

Red Flags in Recruitment Interviews

KNOWING THE DESIRED OUTCOME of a hiring interview is as important as knowing what you do not want. During interviews with prospective salespersons, pay attention to red flags and warning bells.

Mayday Moments

Potential recruits defend and justify a less-than-illustrious event or less-than-brilliant decision. If candidates do this in the interview, they fail to realize they are part of the cause and effect relationship, not outside of it. Do such candidates feel they are victims? ⚑ If so, proceed carefully or come to a full stop.

Some candidates will speak poorly of the competition, peers or management. If they relay negative comments about former associates, they will speak negatively about you and your company. ⚑ Also watch for signs of bitterness and rancor, traits that don't appear on the resume but will indeed follow the employee to your organization. The red flag says *Do Not Hire!*

Question applicants about problems and solutions. Try to determine their attitude toward responsibility for their decisions and the outcomes, and listen for *attitude* warning bells.

Prospective salespeople may want you to make a decision in a hurry, often mentioning competitive job offers. Impatience with process is a liability when selling to Big Game clients. Rushing you to make a quick decision may be a sign of low tolerance levels. Due diligence is vital to senior executives in the decision-making process, and Big Game Hunters won't resort to pressure tactics.

TALK, TELL, TALK, and TELL. If applicants talk non-stop in the interview, how will their customers ever get the chance to ask questions? Lack of consideration is a strong indication of self-centeredness.

How do applicants present themselves? If their appearance is unkempt, do you really want them representing your product or service?

If applicants say *I like people!* does it mean they like cranky customers who demand the world and expect to pay a bargain price?

If applicants say *I am good at solving problems*, ask yourself, if a Big Game Hunter and Closer would make this type of statement? You are probably interviewing a ditherer, a person who gets a thrill from solving problems and may even create a few in order to earn recognition. The Big Game Hunter and Closer foretells, works backwards, and is proactive in preventing problems.

Beware of a Sheep in Wolf's Clothing

Sometimes a sheep dressed like an Alpha wolf applies for a sales position. The CEO and interviewing panel need a due-diligence approach to hiring.

Detection of a sheep in wolf's clothing requires careful discernment. However, the need to be rescued by an apparent Alpha wolf can be overpowering and cloud one's critical judgement. The rewards of a sizzling sales force, one that can rescue the company, may result in hiring impostors 🚩. The sales leader will be inclined to think that the new hire, having produced once, will rise again. It's human nature to hang onto sheep, holding faint, but never-ending hope, when discernment would have chosen a Big Game Hunter and Closer.

An Ounce of Prevention…

There are several steps to mitigate the cycle of hiring the wrong person. Combine a large measure of behavioral interviewing with ongoing willingness to be as objective as possible in the selection process—this is how to avoid costly hiring mistakes.

Don't fall into the trap of hiring in haste. Having an urgent need to fill the position does not mean you take

Impatience with process is a liability when selling to Big Game clients.

the first person who wants the job. It is better for you and the candidate if you take the time to make a good decision.

Here is an important criterion for hiring Alpha Sellers: their eagerness to fill the position should not exceed your need to have it filled.

Behavioral Interviewing

Behavioral interviewing is based on the candidate's job experiences to predict what the candidate will do in similar situations with your company. For instance, a candidate may be asked *to tell me a time when...or can you give me an example when you...?* These questions allow the interviewer to gain valuable insight into the candidate's personality and skillsets. The value of behavioral interviewing techniques is to shed light on past behavior in order to predict future behavior.

Notice the difference in the following questions:

- *Are you willing to prospect and cold call to drive new business?*

- *What percentage of your sales plan now depends on business through prospecting and cold calling?*

The first question allows the candidate to give a yes/ no answer. The second question requires more thought and effort, and lends itself to follow-up elaboration or explanation.

Some salespeople will answer the first question with *Well, I'm not that comfortable with cold calling, but if it's required I'll certainly do my best*. This answer is deceiving. The prospective employee is trying to manage your opinion. Instead of saying *no* to cold calling, which may cause you to view him unfavorably, he says something that sounds like a commitment.

By expanding the question into measurable behaviors around cold calling, the recruiter gets specific information about the candidate's skills. While it is not a perfect tool, this technique provides more insight into your candidate.

Follow-up techniques:

✪ *I'm impressed. Tell me about your system for tracking the numbers from calls to deals.*

✪ *How do you handle objections? Tell me about an objection you encounter when trying to set an appointment or make the deal.*

In my experience, salespeople are not consciously aware of the specific objections they receive, so their responses are not part of a well-thought out system. The exceptions, of course, are the Level 4 and 5 sellers. To get the lion's share of A-list clients, sellers must firmly embrace, explore, and respond to sales objections. (This topic is discussed in greater depth in my book, *Say NO to Me: Secrets of Up$ide-Down Selling*.)

To get the lion's share of A-list clients, sellers must firmly embrace, explore, and respond to sales objections.

Scanning Their Attitudes and Values

From one company to the next, the interview process varies little. As a result, candidates can easily become adept at responding in a manner that manages the process and the interviewer. Their smoothness is less a reflection of their sales expertise, and more a reflection of their experience in the interviewing trenches. If you develop the ability to cull the impostors from the pack, you will save your company hundreds of thousands of dollars in expenses and lost sales opportunities.

The Scanner's Questions

1. *What was your childhood dream?*
2. *Describe your first work experience.*
3. *How important was education in your family?*
4. *Have you ever had a mentor? Tell me about them.*
5. *What is the best business advice you ever received?*
6. *How important is winning?*
7. *How important is money to you?*
8. *Which personal accomplishments give you the greatest pride?*
9. *Which business accomplishments give you the greatest pride?*
10. *Is there one project that stands out for you?*
11. *What is your vision for yourself in five years?*

12. *How do you manage to balance your work and personal life?*

13. *If you could snap your fingers and do one thing to improve the quality of your life, what would that be?*

14. *Let's say you decide to call in for a mental health day tomorrow, how would you spend the day?*

15. *Name one celebrity you would like to meet. Why?*

16. *What do you see in your life's crystal ball?*

17. *If you could choose one thing to do over again, what would it be?*

18. *What do you think of the immigrant situation? Should there be more? Why? Fewer? Why?*

19. *Do you have close friends? Who is your best friend? Why?*

20. *Who are you closer to, your mom or your dad?*

21. *Do you like pets? Dogs best or cats? Why do you prefer [dogs, cats or something else]?*

22. *What makes you feel spontaneous joy?*

23. *Tell me about your favorite movie?*

24. *What do you wish you had never done? Why?*

25. *What do you regret not doing? Why?*

26. *Do you ever feel like everyone else has all of the answers and they forgot to give the rule book to you?*

27. *Describe your experience of working within a team structure.*

28. *Would you be a good manager? Why?*

29. *What are the top three criteria for success?*

...the ability to cull the impostors from the pack will save your company hundreds of thousands of dollars in expenses and lost sales opportunities.

Answers to these questions will reveal much about how well a candidate will fit into your corporate culture. As with all forms of interviewing, there is no perfect answer. If you go after Big Game Hunters and Closers, you will make hiring mistakes. But you will also make your sales team stronger and your bottom line the envy of the industry.

Another Mayday Moment

Positive thinking with no grounding in reality creates happy underachievers. They're happy because they placate themselves with good intentions, magical thinking, and hope. Hope is always about the future. Salespeople who feast on an abundant market place with a belly full of hope will starve to death. The mayday moment comes when the candidate has the zeal of positive thinking but is unable to provide evidence of positive results.

Happy underachievers have the potential to become happy overachievers when they face reality and put an action plan into place. The universe is organized around action. Our planet spins and rotates, the seasons change, and life is continually evolving. I cringe when I hear a salesperson say *I'm putting the energy out there, because what you think about comes to pass*. Yes, positive thoughts are vital, but they must be backed up by appropriate action. Wishing does not make it so, unless you are Alice in Wonderland!

Occasionally life delivers a wake-up call: a moment of change, and we are never the same again. An *epiphany* is often preceded by a loss or hitting bottom, though not necessarily so. At such a time our defences are down, our minds are open, and opportunities suddenly appear. We feel the willingness to do the work, to actualize the opportunity. Life-changing moments depend on your response to the wake-up call.

Positive thinking with no grounding in reality creates happy underachievers.

5

Managing the Super Seller

THERE IS ALWAYS THE THREAT of your competition poaching your star performer. Big Game Hunters and Closers will be less inclined to move if you offer them an equity position in your company. Begin with a small percentage and increase gradually as loyalty and performance become established. It's the *ratchet wrench* approach to building loyalty!

Some Super Sellers expect a signing bonus. It's common practice in professional sport, and now it's entering the game of sales. When Super Sellers request a signing bonus, but their talent is unproven in your field, try switching to a *staying bonus*. The amount of the staying bonus would depend on their overall contribution to the team. Another option is to split the amount between a signing and staying bonus. Big Game Hunters and Closers will likely see this as a win-win negotiation.

Measuring Progress

For a sales team to function fully it must be able to forecast, budget, and plan for future growth. One of the minimum requirements is to have sales methodologies, sales systems, and sales processes in place to measure sales progress. The ability to measure makes it easier to add features, or delete what doesn't work. This is one of the reasons why weekly sales meetings are vital: they are a regular source of feedback from your team to you and from you to your team. Who is better equipped to give you a climate assessment, or fit, of your product or service in the marketplace than those who spend their day in the trenches?

Another Alpha leader technique is to hold every salesperson accountable, including Alpha Sellers. A sales meeting is a public venue for achieving this. It works, because peer opinion is important to the Alpha Seller. Regular sales meetings also provide other members of the team with the opportunity to learn from the Big Game Hunters and Closers. Those at Level 3, craving for more success, want to learn as much as they can as fast as they can from everyone at the meeting. This is most important because Level 3 salespeople are your most likely source of future Level 4 and 5 Super Sellers. With appropriate training send intervention they will 'seed the future' of your company.

A sales meeting should end with what I call *brain food for the salesperson*. Most sales meetings are actually

For a sales team to function fully it must be able to forecast, budget, and plan for future growth.

43

operational in nature, where problems with installation are discussed, budgets are reviewed, and lost deals are lamented. They often close with a Q & A session that drags. But they could close with a presentation by a member of the sales team, a 20-minute talk on an inspirational story or a new sales technique—*brain food*.

Feedback and Trust

An effective method to secure the trust and to manage the sensibilities of Alpha Sellers is to invite feedback and criticism on a regular and casual basis. You can liken this to stepping outside to do a temperature check: you get the feedback and adjust your plans accordingly.

It's simple, but certainly not easy, for managers to solicit feedback. Criticism often triggers our instincts to justify, defend, object, deny, and try to negate the offending situation. But it isn't necessary to try to solve the problem on the spot, or to defend yourself. Disagreement with your idea or request does not mean disapproval of you the person. Instead, provide a noncommittal response that lets the individual know you were listening: *Thanks, I'll have to consider that*.

Believing that they have the private ear of their leader is an inspiration to everyone, not just the positive deviants. Soliciting feedback from your employees is a valuable management technique that works for all members of your sales team, not just your Alpha Sellers. This method is time consuming, but it is time well spent. The time you invest in your sales team pays off in improved motivation and performance, and makes you look good.

Over time, feedback will reveal whom you can count on. It's easy to identify those who find solutions to the problems they talk about, and those who simply complain. You can also identify those who need minor attention to produce better results, as well as those who won't improve regardless of your efforts.

Set Boundaries

While most of your employees do not want to waste your time, a few, given a chance, will demand all of your attention. The solution is to develop and practice techniques that allow you to get their feedback without being drawn into their stories; to set boundaries and stick to them.

Boundaries allow you to deal with people truthfully and still have personal rules. Once your employees know these rules, they will be more comfortable about talking to you. They will know what you can speak about openly and what you are willing to do, and they will accept that. Your boundaries reduce the frustration and resentment that can build from not managing time-wasters. Being a good listener *can* be a wise use of your time and improve the company's bottom line.

The time you invest in your sales team pays off in improved motivation and performance, and makes you look good.

6

Rewarding
Big Game Hunters & Closers

IT HAS BEEN SAID that managing a sales team is about as easy as herding a roomful of cats. In my experience, managing Super Sellers is easier than managing junior or mid-level sellers. Instead of resisting the system, Super Sellers use their energy to drive more and more business.

However, Super Sellers have expectations of their manager. When attempting to resolve issues, they want logic and reason, but not defensiveness.

My first sales job was at Xerox working for Bill Irwin, the sales manager. Bill realized the importance of providing incentives other than compensation packages. Because I was consistently in the top five percent of the sales team, he would assign a new sales associate to work with me in my territory. It helped me become more productive, and the extra incentive helped both Bill and me. I blossomed under his trust in me and his tutelage;

46

I became as devoted to Bill's success as to my own. To help Bill win a Sales Manager's Contest, I submitted sales at the end of one month when it would have served me better to claim in the next month. Conversely, Bill would find subtle ways of alerting me to upcoming sales contests so I could hold back orders that would count towards winning the contest. To this day, I yearn for another mentor like Bill.

Common Mistakes

All too often, CEOs make the mistake of treating Super Sellers as an island unto themselves, totally independent, and fail to provide emotional support or acknowledgment. Too frequently, house accounts and accolades are given to mid- or low-level producers while the Super Seller fumes in silence.

Taking the Alpha Seller for granted is unwise. One leading seller who was making a six-figure income left the company because management continually assigned his lower-dollar clients to new recruits. This former sports professional— without sales experience—had cultivated these clients, but was expected to hand them over to someone else.

Through considerable effort, this Alpha Seller had developed his territory from a zero base to over a million dollars in sales per year. In his way of thinking, new recruits should *earn* their status as salespeople, as he had so ably done. That means putting in the effort to

It has been said that managing a sales team is about as easy as herding a roomful of cats.

learn sales techniques and strategies, to cultivate new clients, and to achieve the satisfaction of generating their own success. He was correct in believing that handing over accounts developed by someone else creates dependency and discourages new recruits from becoming Alpha Sellers.

Management took a different, short-term view of the issue. When the Alpha Seller complained about the pattern, the manager asked him, "How do we keep the rest of our salespeople happy when you make so much more money than they do?" The better question would have been, "How do I teach new recruits to drive their own business?"

As you may have guessed, this company's turnover is high, because when management stopped handing over accounts, the recruits didn't know how to develop their own business. When these junior salespeople move on to other companies, they take credit for their early success and are often hired, only to flounder in mediocrity.

Conclusion: Alpha Sellers expect to be involved in decisions that affect their income and their clients.

However, giving Big Game Hunters and Closers too many breaks and perks can also have negative consequences. Some will become fat cats, curling up and staying, but seeking no further challenge; others become disgruntled and unhappy, which results in their departure for better hunting grounds.

CEOs often fail to sense that their top stars aren't getting the praise and feedback they need. Too many

CEOs do not appreciate the true value of Big Game Hunters, nor understand their sensibilities.

The speed of the leader is the speed of the pack is a proven sales proverb. To manage Super Sellers, the sales manager must understand and practise the principles of the positive deviant. Respecting and rewarding competence are minimal requirements to lead a team of Big Game Hunters and Closers.

Respecting and rewarding competence are minimal requirements to lead a team of Big Game Hunters and Closers.

7

Motivation:
A Highly Personal Matter

IMAGINE A NEW FRANCHISE where you can drop in and buy a quart of motivation. But we know we can't get our motivation topped up by a source outside ourselves. There is no commercial supply because it is impossible to replicate the human will. According to Webster's Dictionary, *to motivate* means "to furnish with a motive, to impel, to induce a person to act in a certain way." *Motive* is defined as "that which incites action; that which determines the choice or moves the will."

That which impels or induces one person to act may not even be of interest to another. Since employers spend the majority of their operating budget on employee wages, they want their employees to be motivated and able to achieve great things. Many systems claim to be fail-proof motivational tools, but, in reality, there are no soft or easy ways to motivate.

One method of motivating is to create a compensation structure in which employees who achieve more are paid more. If asking employees to achieve at a certain level doesn't work, the next step is for the company to show them how to achieve. If after training, an individual remains unproductive, then you could conclude that s/he is truly unmotivated.

Typically, the unmotivated person:

☼ Needs to be given direction for each step of any project.

☼ Is inclined to find fault with the system, the manager and/or the product, but is not inclined to do a self-assessment to find the cause of the problem.

☼ Does not attempt to improve skills in other areas, i.e., resists cross training. They often say *It's not my job* or *That's not in my job description*.

☼ Maintains an indifferent attitude, even if some aspects of their work are quite successful.

☼ Is unresponsive to new ideas and resists change.

☼ Is most comfortable with those who are similarly inclined.

Big Game Hunters and Closers want what they want with desperation; they feel this need to their core.

The Six D's of Success

Big Game Hunters and Closers want what they want with desperation; they feel this need to their core. They also have the ability to detach in a way that allows them to remain focused regardless of the outcome.

When Alpha Sellers fail to have a profitable month, they are quick to perform a self-assessment. They run through an inventory of personal skills and attitudes to see if they lack any of the Six D's of Success—The Motivational Factor:

○ **Detachment**: Pursue your dreams with all your heart, but be prepared to detach from the inevitable setbacks.

○ **Discipline**: Do the right thing because it's the right thing to do, not because it's easy or fun.

○ **Desperation**: Desperation is the unstoppable combination of fear and motivation. Desperation can make one truly willing to do whatever is necessary.

○ **Direction**: Study others and learn from everyone. At the very least, you will learn how not to do something.

✪ **Desire**: Accept that you are a work in progress, and have an honest craving to know, be, and achieve more.

✪ **Determination**: Determination is an unwavering focus on your vision. Understand that you have the right to achieve your dreams. If something has never been done, it simply means *you are the one to do it now*.

Motivation is Highly Personal

Your motivation is highly unique and personal: no one but you can motivate you…it must come from within. The most you can expect from others is to gain inspiration and direction. When you interpret these truths in terms of your own personality, you can increase your desire, determination, desperation, discipline and detachment so that you can achieve more.

When attempting to motivate ourselves or inspire others it is important to remember these points:

1. Destiny is not pre-determined.

2. Every behavior, positive or negative, is purposeful. Ask yourself *What is my purpose in doing/not doing this?*

Your motivation is highly unique and personal: no one but you can motivate you…it must come from within.

3. Our purpose, or that which truly impels us, is often buried or hidden. We need to search within ourselves.

4. There are four typical motivational combinations:

⚙ Determination, desperation, discipline, and detachment

⚙ Determination, desire, discipline, and detachment

⚙ Desire, direction, discipline, and detachment

⚙ Desperation, direction, discipline, and detachment

Changing behavior, even from negative to positive, will generate fear. Fear is the first response to change, even if the change is positive.

As we become more and more willing to move outside our comfort zone, we are rewarded with increased competence and higher performance. What we learn in one area of life, we can transfer to other areas. Increased happiness is the result.

One of the main attributes common to successful employees is the recognition of their own aptitudes, skills, and abilities. The following table presents the attitudes of aptitude of the Big Game Hunter and Closer.

Attitudes of Aptitude

- ✪ **Creativity**: the ability to think of more than one solution.
- ✪ **Stress tolerance**: the ability to manage perceptions of the situation.
- ✪ **Personal insight**: the ability to perceive both strengths and weaknesses.
- ✪ **Communication skills**: the ability to ask questions, listen, and provide feedback.
- ✪ **Self-direction**: the ability to perceive one's self-worth independently of the views of other people, yet be receptive to suggestions for improvement and critical feedback.
- ✪ **Self-motivation**: the ability to look within for energy and initiative, and to be inspired by one's own personal goals and thoughts.
- ✪ **Independence**: the ability to work alone, yet understand the benefit of learning from co-workers; being willing to seek advice knowing that no one has all the answers.
- ✪ **Utilitarian**: the tendency to expect that everything one is involved in is of some value and eventually generates improved outcomes.

Our purpose, or that which truly impels us, is often buried or hidden. We need to search within ourselves.

The Need to Be Inspired

The question that begs to be asked is *Where can inspiration be sourced?* This simple question might be the fuel that ignites all further action. The sources of inspiration are many, and may be mentored (for the lucky few) or self-mentored (for the resilient).

Self-mentoring is the ability to seek ideas and instruction from books, tapes and the history of people who have achieved their dreams. If one person in the world has achieved similar dreams, Big Game Hunters know they can succeed. Even if no one has gone before, they feel confident they can be the first.

Motivation versus Fearful Odds

Continual motivation is the key to success. From personal experience, I know there is more to motivation than the dictionary definition. To achieve our goals, we need *the willingness to feel the pain, to feel discomfort—to pay the price to get the job done*. The most successful people are able to live with fear, uncertainty, and ambiguity, and still move forward. There's more to motivation than positive thinking: we need the ability to move forward in the face of negative thinking, overwhelming fear, discomfort, doubt and insecurity. Positive thinking, without motivation that is grounded in reality, is tantamount to failure.

I have mixed feelings about being introduced as a motivational speaker, because motivation is an inside job. Long-term, sustained motivation must come from an internal source. We can inspire each other through our stories of struggle and survival. We can become *inspired*, but not necessarily *motivated*. Simply stated, motivation is *the willingness to pay the price and feel the pain to reach a goal*. This is the key character trait of the positive deviant—the Alpha Seller, the Super Seller, the Big Game Hunter and Closer.

To achieve our goals, we need the willingness to feel the pain, to feel discomfort—to pay the price to get the job done.

8

The Paradox
of Discomfort and Success

BEING UNABLE TO FUNCTION efficiently while feeling discomfort is a huge hurdle on the road to success. The main goal in life is to avoid discomfort and to protect our vulnerable selves. The paradox is *the more we seek to avoid discomfort the more ineffective we become*.

Failing to ask for the order, failing to go above the level of the contact (even though the contact is unable to approve the contract) and failing to confront peers, colleagues and clients, are examples of protecting feelings in order to avoid discomfort. This sounds simple enough to change, as if one could just say *Okay, I'll pull the switch and change*. However, it is neither simple nor easy; if it were, there would be more Alpha Sellers. True success depends on the ability to remain focused, and to pursue goals in the face of emotional discomfort.

When is the best time to start living outside the comfort zone? Today! Acknowledge that it's neither easy nor simple, and be willing to feel the discomfort—one percent per day. Remember the Carlos case study? He worked hard every day to overcome his fear and doubt, and he achieved great results.

The Confidence Myth

Too many people believe the popular philosophers: that self-confidence and self-esteem are the answer. So much for philosophy! When people feel a knot in their stomach or trepidation in their heart, they assume that they alone feel this way. They believe it means they lack self-confidence, when it really means they lack experience.

No matter how badly you want it, it is impossible to feel confidence before you achieve competence. Experience generates competence, which eventually leads to confidence. Countless people berate themselves because they fail to recognize and understand that competence, not confidence, is the answer. Achieving competence without uncomfortable feelings is like trying to breathe without being born.

Progress, Not Perfection

The second hurdle on the road to becoming a Super Seller is to stop striving for perfection. Perfectionists continue to do, over and over again, what they already know how to do. Show me a perfectionist and I'll show you a procrastinator.

No matter how badly you want it, it is impossible to feel confidence before you achieve competence. Experience generates competence, which eventually leads to confidence.

The seeds of perfection were planted when we were children. Over and over again, we were berated and admonished with this: *A job worth doing is worth doing well*. Many children believe they can't do anything right and begin to fear failure and criticism.

In his hit song *On the Way to the Sky*, Neil Diamond sings about the futile search for perfection:

> *We pity the poor one*
> *The shy and unsure one*
> *Who wanted it perfect*
> *But waited too long*

Alpha Sellers know they must be willing:

○ to make mistakes;

○ to lose clients because they were too zealous;

○ to call the CEO shaking with fear;

○ to embrace objections rather than avoid them;

○ to offer new ideas and differing strategies to the team;

○ not to wait for perfect timing.

A case in point involves my own cold-calling experience. Although my track record is impressive, I make mistakes. Sometimes I get off the phone, put my head on my desk and ask myself, *How could I have said that? Why did I talk so fast? How could I interrupt her three times?* All of this happens, but so what?

If we obsess over mistakes, we paralyze ourselves and halt our forward movement. When we make a mistake we need to practise saying, *Oops! Next...* People must be willing face their imperfections and feel uncomfortable in the process. The secret to progress is a paradox: *Anything worth doing is worth doing imperfectly*. To be more successful, we must be willing to make more mistakes.

Consistently Consistent

The third and equally important hurdle is consistency. A poor marketing plan diligently implemented will yield far greater results than an exemplary marketing plan implemented occasionally. Any product or service that is not sold quickly becomes a burden. Most entrepreneurs and businesses have a product or service niche. They are expert in their field, and assume prosperity will come when the word spreads about their perfect product or brilliant service. However, if they don't get the word out, they will surely fail. The way to get the word out is to be diligent and *consistent* in setting a portion of every day for cold calling and prospecting.

Anything worth doing is worth doing imperfectly. To be more successful, we must be willing to make more mistakes.

9

Prospect and Prosper

THOSE WHO PROSPECT THE MOST, sell the most. For product-oriented companies, five self-respectful, customer-respectful cold calls a week, per salesperson, will drive enough business to reach any goal. This may sound like an outlandish statement, but it is true—with one proviso: the cold calls must be initiated with a script containing my *million-dollar principles* and built upon the personality of the seller. They are million-dollar principles because by using them consistently to attract new clients you will create financial success.

The Million-Dollar Script

One of my biology professors used to say *A word to the wise is sufficient*. Ben Franklin said it another way: *The wise learn from their own experiences. The truly intelligent learn from someone else's*. As you read this, I can imagine some of you saying, "I don't believe in scripts," or "I don't want my salespeople using scripts." Nevertheless, you do!

If I were to follow anyone for three calls, I'd know exactly what they were going to say on the fourth call. Everyone uses a script now, one that is designed for the caller's peace of mind, personality, and comfort zone. A good script must be consistently implemented in an imperfect fashion. Several elements are necessary to win the attention, respect, and receptivity of the contact in the first ten seconds.

An Alpha Seller already knows never to say *How are you today?* Nothing is more effective in establishing you as an ordinary and a mundane salesperson than if you begin your call with that insincere question. A good script contains all of the following million-dollar principles.

Million-Dollar Principles

The **first** principle is to create alignment and receptivity, instead of oppositional thinking and resentment, during the first ten seconds of the prospecting/cold call. When you phrase your opening statement to establish this, the prospect begins listening instead of thinking. Thinking allows them to distance themselves from your agenda by wondering *Who is she? What does she want? Where did she get my name?* It's important to answer those mental questions immediately by saying, "Hello, my name is [insert your name], we've never met, and the reason I'm calling…"

The **second** principle is to *wound* the prospect—gently. You can do this only if you know the problems

…create alignment and receptivity, instead of oppositional thinking and resentment, during the first ten seconds of the prospecting/cold call.

you can solve for your client. It amazes me when I ask participants in my workshops to list four problems their product or service can solve for their clients, and they don't know the answer.

The **third** principle is to offer a Band-Aid, or solution, for the wound or problem.

The **fourth** is to prevent oppositional defiance by giving them a legitimate choice to say no three times. This can be done so subtly that prospects aren't consciously aware of it, but they are very aware subconsciously and listen with interest all the way through your presentation.

The **fifth** principle is to solicit, expect, receive, and embrace objections. There are only four objections you will encounter during a call. Two are standard and two are from industry. If you know them, it's easy to handle them. When I teach this in my workshops, participants look positively gleeful, anticipating how they will outfox the next cold-calling prospect!

(My book, *Say NO to Me: Secrets of Up$ide-Down Selling*, covers, in depth, how to handle objections. Specific scripts and strategies explaining how to use objections to get the deal are included.)

The **sixth** principle is to ask three times for the appointment. Your chances increase 25% with each asking. Each time you ask, you demonstrate you're one of the Alpha Sellers and not likely to waste their time with smooth chit-chat. Big Game clients will follow a decisive salesperson.

The **seventh** principle is to understand and apply the knowledge that people are motivated to practice enlightened self-interest. Everyone likes to believe in and project an image of being a fair person. Knowing this, if you close your request for an appointment or a concession by asking *Does this sound fair to you?* clients will try to uphold a positive image of themselves by replying yes.

The **eighth** principle is to practice an attitude of discipline and detachment. (See *The Six D's of Success* in Chapter 7.) Want what you want with all your heart and soul. Get up every morning with fire in your belly and throw gasoline on it. Do your absolute fervent best and then—detach from the outcome. When you can do this, you will not take rejection personally. Just say to yourself, *So what? Next!*

GoalsGutsGlory

Following is a script drawing on these eight principles. When I make ten qualified calls, I get eight appointments. My qualification process is simple. I speak to the CEO or Vice President of Sales, and I make sure that they have budgetary approval. I always speak slowly and in a measured way because if my prospects interrupt me, it tells me they are interested and wish to engage with me about their buying issues. Indifference is a kiss of death.

Most people will make a cold call planning to be nice, non-threatening and agreeable. Most people are average,

…understand and apply the knowledge that people are motivated to practice enlightened self-interest.

and they achieve average results. While customers are not always nice, non-threatening or agreeable, they always have the right to be heard with respect.

A prospect might offer this objection: "I don't need sales training because my whole team was 15% over sales quota last year." An average sales trainer would say, "Oh, that's great. Thank you very much for your time" and hang up. Not me. I'd say, "Well, how do you know they couldn't have achieved 20% or more?" And an Alpha sales leader wouldn't sit on his laurels. He'd reply, "You're right. Maybe they could. Let's meet and see if there's more sales capacity in my team."

The following script contains a number of "black flags" and "white flags." The black flags show the points in the conversation when the prospect feels anxiety. The lowered white flags indicate places in the script where your comments have reduced the anxiety. The black flags are offset by the white flags, resulting in the presence of overall creative tension. Do not assume that the conversation must be pleasant and agreeable. Creative tension is a desirable component of any prospecting conversation.

Win or Lose...

An arrogant salesperson expects to win every time. *Why would anyone think it's possible to go through life without disappointment, loss and failure?* People have a natural tendency to structure their lives to minimize setbacks.

Million-Dollar Script

Hello, my name is [insert your name] (◣) and we've never met (◹). The reason I'm calling (◹) is that I understand you're the person in charge of sales training for your company (◣). Is this true or has someone been spreading a rumor (◹)? Let me tell you, (◣) if that's all right with you, (◹) what I do and you can tell me if our businesses would be a match (◹). Let me ask you a question: As sales manager, do you always intend to spend time with your salespeople, but your time is so limited that you're never quite able to keep that commitment…to yourself (◣ ◣ ◣)?

What we could do, (◣) if that's okay with you, (◹) is set a time to meet and discuss how my company supports the expectations of a sales manager like you, who wants it done just right, but doesn't have the time (◹). Then you tell me if we're a match or not. Does that sound fair to you? (◹).

When they do this, they miss out on the opportunity and thrill of winning big.

This book has provided you with an overview of the nature of Big Game Hunters and Closers, the Alpha Sellers, the Super Sellers—also known as Positive Deviants. Top sellers are vital to your sales team so that your company can secure more A-list accounts. The

Creative tension is a desirable component of any prospecting conversation.

A-list clients are buying from someone. It may as well be you. Let's review the traits of a Super Seller, a Big Game Hunter and Closer.

Dance Like a Bee

Everyone has heard the expression, *He made a beeline for...* The word *beeline* refers to the behavior of a bee that finds nectar. That bee comes directly back to the hive and performs a dance, which reveals the exact location of the nectar. Most of the other bees fly off in this direction, locate the nectar and come back with an abundant supply. However, 20% of the bees fly off in different directions, find other *new* sources of nectar and return to the hive to perform a new dance for their teammates. If every bee rushed off to the same flowers, the resource would quickly be depleted. The group of deviant bees, flying off in new directions, is exactly what is needed for the hive to live long and prosper.

Having Super Sellers on your team is somewhat similar. The Super Seller often doesn't follow the directions to common sources. They are destined to forage, and even scavenge, if necessary, to meet their own as well as company goals. Super Sellers are the positive deviants who keep topping up the sales budget for the sales manager and the CEO.

Conclusion

BIG GAME HUNTERS AND CLOSERS, the sellers with Alpha-leader traits, can be bought or built. A company that invests the time and money to develop their own Super Sellers will have the unstoppable combination of sales leadership and loyalty. That combination will make your sales team stronger and your bottom line the envy of the industry.

How to Reach Us

To book Alice Wheaton, for a keynote, half-day or full-day presentation, please contact her, toll free in North America, at **1(877) 542•5423**. To review other video, audio and text resources by Alice Wheaton, please visit her website at **http://www.alicewheaton.com**

CoreGrowth Foundations Inc.
Suite 1844, Westhills Town Center
Calgary, Alberta T3H 3C8
CANADA
Toll Free: 1 (877) 542•5423
Phone: (403) 249•5853
Fax: (403) 249•3514
E-mail: awheaton@alicewheaton.com

Jellicle Ball Publishing Company
is an imprint of CoreGrowth Foundations Inc.